The Boys' Guide to Growing Up

Choices & Changes during Puberty

Terri Couwenhoven, M.S.

Woodbine House 2012

All illustrations (except on pages 3, 20, 33, 55) by Gary Mohrman.

Library of Congress Cataloging-in-Publication Data

Couwenhoven, Terri.
  The boys' guide to growing up : choices & changes during puberty / Terri Couwenhoven. -- 1st ed.
      p. cm.
  Includes index.
  ISBN 978-1-60613-089-6
  1. Teenage boys--Physiology--Juvenile literature. 2. Sex instruction for children with mental disabilities. 3. Puberty--Juvenile literature. I. Title.
  RJ143.C68 2012
  613'.04233--dc23

                                                    2012025776

Manufactured in the United States of America

10 9 8 7

This book is dedicated to
the boys and their parents in my
puberty workshops who taught me that
understandable information
is a powerful thing.

Table of Contents

Note to Parents..vii

Puberty Basics
★ What Is Puberty?.. 2
★ When Will You Begin Puberty?................... 4

Outside Changes
★ Changes in Your . . . Growth 6
★ Changes in Your . . . Private Parts.............. 8
★ Hair, Hair, Everywhere! 9
★ Changes in Your . . . Skin........................... 11

Inside Body Changes
★ Changes in Your . . . Voice..........................16
★ Changes in Your . . . Feelings.....................17
★ Changes in . . . Sexual Feelings..................19

About Your Penis
★ What Is an Erection? 28
★ What Is an Ejaculation? 31

Handling Yourself around Others

★ Handling Yourself around Others............36
★ Keeping Yourself Safe................................38

Public or Private

★ What Are the Private Body Parts? 46
★ Public or Private?...47

Final Words

★ Growing Up Is Normal! 52
★ Growing Up Is Normal! 53

Index 61

About the Author..64

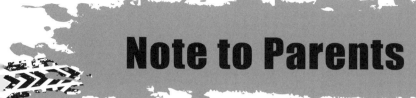

Note to Parents

As the parent of a child with a developmental disability, you are probably used to your child needing extra time to accomplish things. For many parents, it is surprising to find that their son's physical development and initiation into puberty is right on schedule!

This book is specifically designed to help boys with developmental disabilities understand what to expect during puberty. Because this resource is for people who typically struggle with reading comprehension and/or social cues, it presents information differently than other books about puberty. Differences include:

★ **Lower Reading Level**—Although the content is geared toward boys who are chronologically aged about 11 to 15, the words and descriptions are targeted to a third-grade reading level.

★ **Visual Cues**—This book contains lots of clear illustrations to emphasize information being described in the text and enhance comprehension.

★ **Content**—The scope of information in this book is narrower and more focused on the needs of people with developmental disabilities. My goal for the book is to introduce your son to male body changes that happen during puberty and to help him know how to handle them. The content I selected is based on over 15 years of feedback from families like yours who have attended my parent/child puberty workshops.

★ **Language**—The language is simple and unsophisticated. When appropriate, slang terminology has been added in parentheses. It is well known that individuals with intellectual disabilities are often more familiar with slang terms than the language you might hear in the doctor's office. I wanted readers to have a frame of reference for various types of language. You can share your own views about the language you prefer your son to use.

Depending on your son's personality, learning style, or reading level, you may want to read this book together. People with developmental disabilities struggle a bit more with framing questions and voicing concerns. I hope this book can be a catalyst for helping you to talk directly and openly with your son about a sensitive subject. There will be additional sexuality topics (not addressed in this book) your son will need help understanding. By initiating discussions with your son now, you are modeling for him the importance of talking about sexuality. And being viewed by your son as a safe and approachable resource now and in the future is indeed a good thing!

Best Wishes,

Terri Couwenhoven

Puberty
Basics

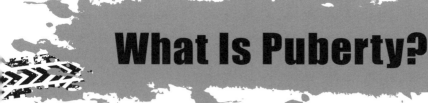

What Is Puberty?

This book will help you get ready for an important time in your life. This time is called **puberty**.

Puberty is the time when kids begin to grow up. During puberty, your body will change. Some changes will make you **look** more like a man. Other changes will make you **feel** more like a man.

The changes that happen are normal and happen to everyone!

Both boys and girls go through puberty. But this book is just about changes that happen to boys.

Look at the picture of the boy and the man on the next page. Can you see how their bodies are different?

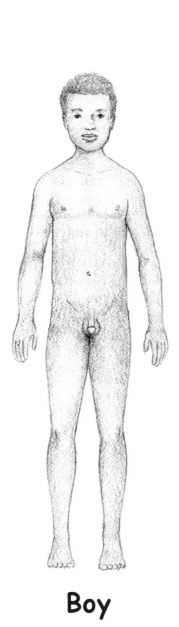

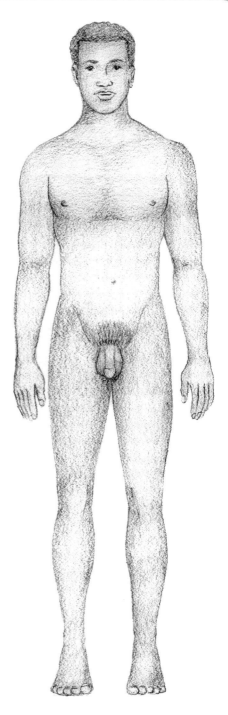

Boy   **Man**

When Will You Begin Puberty?

The short answer is: between age 9 and 15. That's when most boys **start** puberty.

Here's the long answer:

Puberty will start when your body is ready. That might be when you are 10 or 11. Or you might be a little older—age 12 or 13. Or you might not see any changes until age 14 or 15.

Your body will change at its own speed. It will take a few years before you look like a grown man.

Let's talk about the ways your body will change during puberty.

Outside Changes

What Changes Will You See?

Body changes you can see are called outside changes. When you see these changes, it means you are starting puberty.

Changes in your. . . GROWTH

During puberty your body will grow in many ways!

★ You will get taller and you will need larger clothes.

★ Your feet will grow and you will need bigger shoes.

★ Your shoulders will get wider and you will notice more muscles.

These body changes are normal. They happen to all boys during puberty.

It will take a few years for your body to stop growing and changing. When puberty is over, you will look like a man.

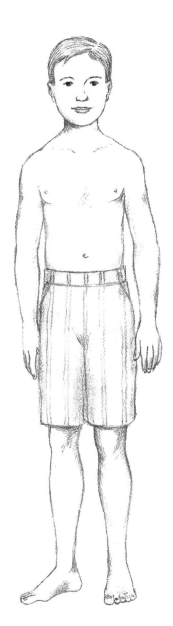

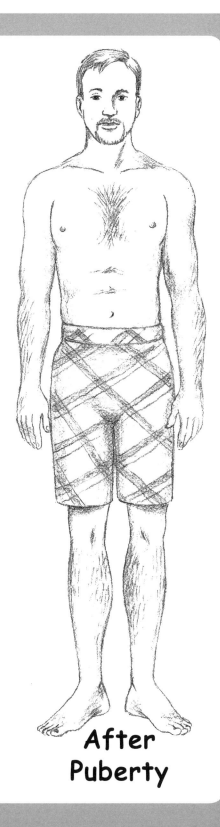

Before
Puberty

After
Puberty

Changes in your...
PRIVATE PARTS

During puberty, the private parts between your legs will start to grow too! These parts are called the penis and testicles (or balls).

Some boys worry about the size of their penis. Is it too small? Is it too long? Everyone is different, though. Your penis will grow to be the size that's right for you.

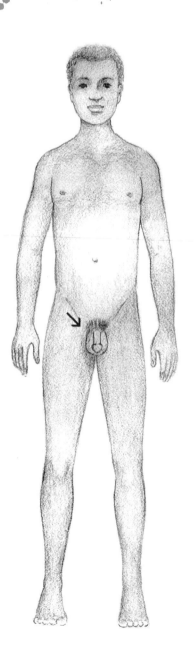

Hair, Hair, Everywhere!

During puberty, you will grow more hair. Hair will grow in new places on your body. It will grow in places where you never had hair before.

Hair will grow on the private area between your legs. Hair that grows here is called pubic hair.

Hair will also grow in your armpits.

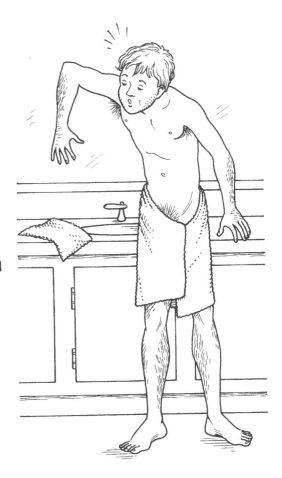

PRIVATE It is normal to find pubic and underarm hair. But it is private! If you have questions about your new hair, only talk to your parent or another adult you trust.

Hair will also grow on your face. You will see hair above your lip and on your chin. The hair on your face is not private but public. Public means it's okay for other people to see the hair that grows on your face.

At first the hair on your face will grow slowly. As you get older, it will grow faster.

If you don't shave the hair on your face, guess what you will have? A beard or a mustache!

If you do not want hair on your face, you will need to shave.

Learning how to shave takes practice. Your parents can teach you how to use a shaver. Shaving the hair on your face can help you look clean.

Changes in your...
SKIN

During puberty, you might see changes in your skin. Your face might get more oily or shiny. It might also get red bumps or sores called pimples (zits or acne). Some boys get pimples on their back, chest, or other body parts too.

It's important to keep your skin clean. Wash your face in the morning when you get up and at night before bed. Try not to touch or squeeze pimples.

If the pimples hurt or won't go away, talk to your doctor.

What's That Smell?

Skin changes can make you smell different too! Body odor (or B.O.) gets stronger during puberty.

What can you do so you won't stink?

★ Wash your armpits and private parts.

★ Bathe more often.

★ Use deodorant.

Most boys start to use deodorant during puberty. Rub some in your armpits and you won't sweat so much. It helps you smell better too!

There are many kinds of deodorant. Some rub on dry. Others rub on wet. They all smell different too. You can decide if you want to smell like soap, spices, or just your natural you!

If you smell bad, people won't want to be near you. To stop smells, wash your body and use deodorant every day.

Inside Body Changes

Changes won't just happen on the outside of your body. There will be inside changes too. You can't see these changes. But you might start to feel different.

Let's talk about changes that happen inside your body during puberty.

Changes in your... VOICE

During puberty, your voice will change. You will start out with a higher voice, like a kid. As you grow, your voice will get lower and more like a man's voice.

While your voice is changing, it might not sound like you want it to. It might sound squeaky. Some boys get embarrassed if their voice squeaks. But voice changes are normal and happen to all boys.

Changes in your... FEELINGS

During puberty, your feelings or moods can change a lot. One minute you may feel happy. The next minute, you may feel angry or sad. This is called being **moody**.

Feeling moody is normal. It happens to all boys during puberty.

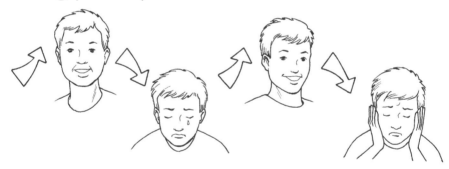

Handling Your Moods

Part of growing up is learning how to handle your feelings. When you feel moody, here are some things you can do:

★ Spend time doing fun things. Listen to music or watch a favorite TV show. What do you like to do to have fun?

★ Move your body! Playing sports, walking, or dancing can help you feel better when you are having a bad day.

★ Take time to be by yourself. Having private time away from other people can help.

★ Write about your feelings or talk with someone you trust.

Changes in...
SEXUAL FEELINGS

During puberty, you might have new and exciting feelings when you see or think about someone you like. This is called **having sexual feelings** or **having a crush**.

Some boys have crushes on TV and movie stars. Other boys have crushes on people at school or in the community. Some boys don't have these feelings at all. That's normal too!

Handling Crushes

Some teens flirt with people they have crushes on. **Flirting** means you do things to let the person know that you like them.

Some teens flirt by **talking** to the person they like. They might talk about safe things like movies or music. It's good to see if you have things in common with the person you like. It can feel good to talk to a person you have a crush on.

Other teens flirt by **doing something** to show the person they like them. They write notes, text, smile, stare, or move closer to the person.

It's OK if you are too shy to talk to the person you like. You can keep your feelings private. You can write about your feelings in a private journal. This is another way to handle sexual feelings.

Rules for Flirting

Flirting can be fun. But there are rules you need to know:

1. Only flirt with people who are about your same age.

2. Do not flirt with adults (teachers, aides, store clerks, bus drivers, waiters, or waitresses).

3. Do not flirt when you need to be working or learning.

4. Sometimes the person you like will not like you back. This happens to everyone.

If a person you like does not like you back, they might:

★ Act like they don't want to talk to you

★ Ignore you

★ Make excuses for why they can't talk or be with you

★ Never return messages

If this happens, it means the person does not like you back, so you should STOP FLIRTING.

PRIVATE Having sexual feelings and crushes is normal. When a person you have a crush on does not like you back, it is best to keep your feelings to yourself. If you have questions, talk to your parent or a safe adult you trust.

Sweethearts & Dating

When you are old enough, you may want to have a sweetheart. Sweethearts like each other very much. Often they have sexual feelings for each other. They also have things in common.

Sweethearts spend time together dating. Dating helps them find out if they are a good match for each other.

Talking about sexual feelings with a sweetheart is normal and healthy. Sweethearts can say private things like: "You are beautiful" or "You are so much fun to be with" or "I like you a lot."

Not everyone has a sweetheart. That's OK too! It can take a long time to find a person who is a good match.

What *Else* Can You Do about Sexual Feelings?

Some boys touch or rub their private body parts when they are alone. They do this when they have sexual feelings or think about someone they like. This can feel good.

Touching or rubbing your own private body parts is called **masturbation.** For more information about what happens when you masturbate, see page 32.

Some boys do not like to touch their private parts. That is OK too. (See page 46 if you are not sure which body parts are private.)

PRIVATE Touching your penis, testicles, or butt is very **private.** (That's why they are called private parts!) Make sure you are in your bedroom or bathroom at home with the door closed.

What Is an Erection?

When you have sexual feelings, your penis might get harder and longer. (It seems to "grow.") This is called having an **erection**. (Guys call it a **hard-on** or **boner**.) During puberty, the penis can get hard more often. Sometimes it seems to get hard for no reason at all!

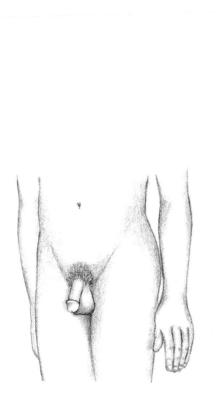

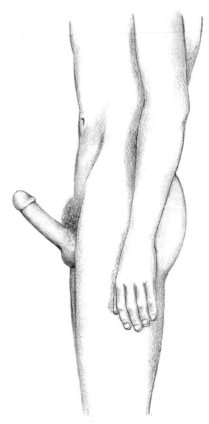

Penis

This is an erection

Erections Are Private!

PRIVATE Erections are normal. They happen to all boys. But having an erection is **private**. Keep information about your erection (or penis) to yourself.

Handling Erections

If you have an erection and you are around other people, try to keep it private! Do not touch or rub your penis. Do not tell others around you what is happening to your body.

Here are some things you **can** do until the erection goes away:

* At school, walk to your desk and sit down.

* At home, sit in a chair. Other people will not be able to tell you have an erection if you are sitting down.

* Wear longer shirts that cover the area between your legs.

* Hide your erection with a sweatshirt, backpack, or books as you walk.

* Try to think about food, hobbies, or work you are supposed to be doing.

If you leave your penis alone, your erection **will** go away on its own.

What Is an Ejaculation?

Before puberty, only one thing comes out of a boy's penis—urine (pee). At the end of puberty, another liquid can come out too! This liquid is called semen. (This is **not** the same as people who work at sea. Those are SEAmen.)

Semen is a whitish, sticky liquid. It is made by inside body parts you can't see. These body parts start to work during puberty.

When semen comes out of the penis it is called **ejaculation** (or **coming**).

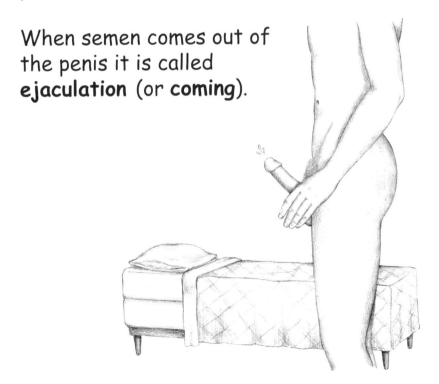

Once your body starts making semen, you can have an ejaculation. (Semen can squirt out of your penis.) But you have to **do** something to make the semen come out. It doesn't come out on its own.

One way to ejaculate is to touch or rub your penis. (See **masturbation** on page 25.) Touching or rubbing your penis will make it get hard. (Do you remember what it's called when the penis gets hard?) If you keep rubbing, semen will come out. When the semen comes out, it feels good. It can make a teen feel relaxed.

After semen comes out, you need to clean your body. Keep some wet wipes near your bed. Or wash your penis and hands when you are done.

Some boys and men masturbate when they bathe. That way they can clean their bodies when they are done.

Ejaculations Are Private!

PRIVATE

Ejaculations are normal. They happen to all boys. But masturbation and ejaculations are **private**. Do not talk to others about your penis and what you do in private.

What Is a Wet Dream?

Some mornings you may wake up and see wet spots on your bed sheets. This is called having a **wet dream**. A wet dream just means semen came out of your penis (or you ejaculated) while you were sleeping.

If you notice you had a wet dream, put your sheets and pajamas in the wash. Or tell your mom or dad they need to be washed.

Wet dreams are normal. They can happen when your inside body parts begin to work like a man's.

PRIVATE

Wet dreams are normal. They happen to all boys. But they are private. Keep information about wet dreams to yourself. If you have questions, you can talk to your mom or dad or another safe adult.

Handling Yourself around Others

Handling Yourself around Others

Once you begin puberty, it means you are growing up! This is a good time to start practicing to be an adult. Part of being an adult is knowing how to take care of your body and manage your feelings.

Look at the list on the next page. Try to match the body change with the picture that shows what you should do if this happens:

Mix & Match!

If this happens:	**I should:**
 I have oily skin and zits.	 Keep my feelings private.
 I have body odor.	 Shave.
 I have hair on my face.	 Take a shower.
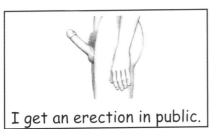 I get an erection in public.	 Wash my face.
 I have a crush on someone who doesn't feel the same way.	 Try to hide the erection and keep private.

Keeping Yourself Safe

You are growing up and learning to be an adult now. Part of being an adult is learning rules about your body. These rules will help you be safe at home and in public.

Rules for Your Body and Private Body Parts

Now that you are becoming a man, you need to be **modest**. This means keeping your private body parts covered when you are around people.

If you are not sure which body parts are private, look at page 46.

Here are some rules:

★ Keep your clothes on when you're in public.

★ Wear a robe or towel when you walk from the bathroom to your bedroom after bathing.

★ Close your bedroom door when you are changing clothes.

★ In the bathroom at home, close the door when you are doing things that are private.

★ In a locker room, don't stare at other people's bodies. And always keep your hands to yourself.

★ In a public bathroom, use the urinal farthest away from anyone. Keep your eyes on where you are peeing. Keep your hands to yourself. Others should not look or touch you. If you want more privacy, go in a stall and close the door.

PRIVATE Remember, your body is private and belongs to you.

Touching Rules for Your Body

You get to decide when and if you want to be touched.

If someone touches you and you don't want to be touched, you can shout:

★ "NO!"

★ "STOP!" or

★ "I DON'T LIKE THAT!"

Or, you can use your body to let someone know you don't want to be touched. You can:

★ Put your hand up to say "stop."

★ Shake your head "no."

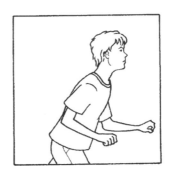

★ Walk away.

IMPORTANT: There are a few times (only two) when people may need to touch you even if you don't want to be touched. This might happen if your body or private parts need care.

Can you think of examples?

People Who Can Touch or Look at Your Body

1. **Your doctor or a nurse.**
   Your doctor or nurse might need to look at you when you are undressed. He or she might need to touch or check your private parts. A doctor's job is to check your body to make sure it is healthy. This includes your private parts.

2. **Your mom, dad, or another adult helper.**
   Keeping your body clean is part of growing up. Some boys need help learning how to clean their bodies. While you are learning, it is OK for your parent or another safe person to help you clean yourself. Your parents will tell you who can help you with hygiene if you need help.

   If you can clean your body by yourself, other people do not need to be in the bathroom with you. Ask for privacy. You can say: "Privacy, please" or "I will tell you if I need help."

REMEMBER: Only your doctor, nurse, parent, or adult helper can look at or touch your private parts. It is not OK for anybody else to see or touch them.

If this happens, you should:

Say "No!"

Get away.

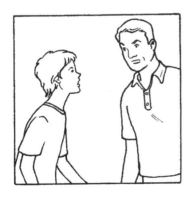

Tell an adult who will listen.

Rules for Touching Others

Not everybody likes to be touched. Sometimes people you are trying to hug might say no or back away. That means they don't want to be touched.

If you meet someone for the first time, you can shake hands and say "Nice to meet you." This is what people do if they are meeting someone new.

It is not OK to touch or hug people you do not know.

It is never OK to touch or look at another person's private body parts. If someone asks you to look at or touch their private body parts, you should:

Say "No!"	Get away.	Tell an adult.

What Are the Private Body Parts?

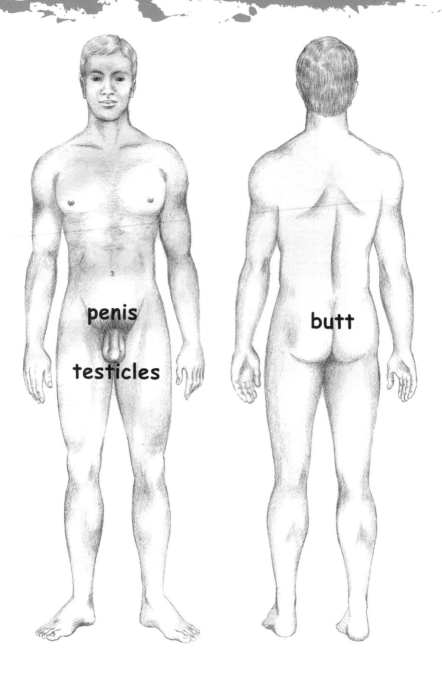

penis

butt

testicles

Public or Private?

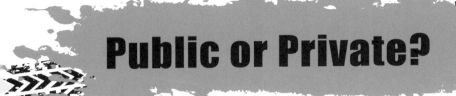

Once puberty is over, you will look like an adult (not a little boy). When you look like an adult, people will want you to act like a grown-up. So, you need to learn grown-up rules for what you can say and do in public and private.

Let's review what these two words mean:

PUBLIC means that other people are around. Can you think of one of your favorite public places?

public

PRIVATE means that you are alone. Nobody can see or hear you. Do you have a private place at home? What is it?

private

Public and Private Quiz

Here is a list of things that many of us do
Seven of them should only be done in private.
Do you know which ones?

DIRECTIONS:
If a sentence talks about something private,
circle the bold letter in the sentence. Then
write down the letters on a piece of paper. Do
the letters spell a word?

1. Touch your **P**enis. Is this public or private?

2. **A**sk where the restroom is. Is this public or private?

3. Eat an **I**ce cream cone. Is this public or private?

4. **R**ub deodorant under your arms. Is this public or private?

5. Watch a **M**ovie with kissing in it. Is this public or private?

6. Share **I**nformation about your body changes. Is this public or private?

7. Play video **G**ames. Is this public or private?

8. Buy **D**eodorant at the store. Is this public or private?

9. Scratch your penis when it is **V**ery itchy. Is this public or private?

10. **A**sk a question about wet dreams. Is this public or private?

11. **T**ake a shower. Is this public or private?

12. Tell a knock-knock **J**oke. Is this public or private?

13. Have an **E**rection. Is this public or private?

14. Listen to **M**usic. Is this public or private?

Answer (Turn upside down!)

The private things are in sentences 1, 4, 6, 9, 10, 11, and 13. They spell the word **private**.

Growing Up is Normal!

It is exciting to change from a boy to a man. But it can also be a little scary. It is normal to have questions about what is going on!

When you have questions, talk to a parent or another adult you trust. Other people don't need to know what is happening to your body. Remember, body changes are **private.**

Puberty is normal. It happens to all boys. It's part of growing up!

Questions & Answers about the Body, Sexual Feelings & Growing Up

1. What causes erections?

When you have sexual feelings, blood from inside the body fills the veins and arteries in the penis. When blood moves into the penis, the penis gets bigger.

Some boys and men get an erection when they have to pee. When your bladder is full of pee, it can cause the penis to get hard. In this case, peeing will make the erection go away.

2. What if I'm not at home when I get an erection?

It is hard to know when you will get an erection. But if you feel your penis getting hard, try to keep others from noticing.

Things to try:
  ★ Sit down if you can. If you are walking at school, go to your next class and sit down. People will not notice if you are sitting down.

* Wear longer shirts or untuck your shirt so your shirt covers your crotch area. People will not be able to tell you have an erection.

* Wear stiffer pants like jeans. Stiffer pants make it harder for the penis to move.

* Try to think about other things. Try thinking about food you like, what you will do when you get home, music, people in TV shows, etc.

* If you are at the pool or beach, put a towel over your lap to hide your erection. Getting into cold water can help an erection go away too!

3. **Is it scary to have a wet dream?**
It might be a little scary when you have your first wet dream. That's because you don't know when it will happen. And it is something new and different for you. Having a wet dream does not hurt.

This book was made to help you learn all about body changes. This will help you know what can happen so you are not afraid.

Remember, all boys go through these changes. It is a sign that your body is healthy and working like it should.

4. What is the difference between pee and semen?

Urine (or pee) is yellowish and clear. It comes from an inside body part called the bladder. How much you pee is connected to how much you drink.

Semen is white and sticky. It is made in different places inside the body. Semen also has sperm in it, which is needed to make babies. See the next question for more on this.

5. Why do boys and men ejaculate?

Men (and boys going through puberty) make sperm inside their bodies. These sperm look like tiny tadpoles and are in the semen. Sperm are very small—too small to see with the naked eye.

Sperm is one of the two things needed to make a baby. The other thing is an egg from inside a woman's body.

A baby can be made when sperm from inside the man's body is joined with an egg from inside the woman's body. Ejaculation is the main way sperm gets out of the man's body to meet the egg from the woman's body. Some grown-up couples decide to have a baby when they feel they can handle the work of taking care of another person.

6. **Can I stop my sexual feelings?**
No. Sexual feelings (or crushes) are normal and happen to everyone. What you do with these feelings will depend on where you are and who you are with.

Remember, sexual feelings are private most of the time. It is OK to talk about your feelings:

★ when you are talking to one of your parents in private

★ when you are talking to someone who feels the same way about you

7. When can I start dating?

There is no magic age that it is okay to date. Some teens begin dating in high school. Others wait until they are adults. It is hard to know when you will meet the right person.

Here is the most important thing to know about dating: The person you like must also like you. A sweetheart relationship can only start when **both** people have sexual feelings for each other.

8. Why do people date?

Dating is how two people get to know each other better. Spending time together helps couples learn if they are a good match for each other.

9. What does it mean when a girl says, "I like you as a friend"?

When a girls says this it means:

★ She does not have sexual feelings for you.

★ She does not want you to flirt with her.

★ She does not want to be your girlfriend.

★ She does not want to go on dates with you.

These words mean she feels safer if you treat her like a friend, not a sweetheart. When a girl tells you this it means you should keep your sexual feelings to yourself.

If someone likes you as a friend, it means:

★ You can still say "hi" when you see her.

★ You can talk about safe things like:
Music, TV shows, Sports, Classes

★ You might spend time together in a group.

Index

Acne, 11
Adult, looking like, 2, 6, 47
Balls, 8
Bathrooms, public, 39
Before and after pictures, 3, 7
Body change quiz, 37
Body odor (B.O.), 12-13
Butt, 25, 46
"Coming," 31
Crushes, 19-22, 56
Dating, 23-24, 57
Deodorant, 12
Doctors, 42
Ejaculation, 31-32, 55
Erections, 28-30, 53-54
Facial hair, 10
Feelings, 17-18
Feet, 6
Flirting, 20-22
Friends vs. sweethearts, 57-58
Growth, changes in, 6
Hair on the body, 9
Hair on the face, 10
Height, 6

Hugging, 44
Hygiene
    after ejaculation, 32
    getting help, 42
    keeping face clean, 11
    preventing odors, 12-13
Man, changing into, 2, 6, 47
Masturbation, 25, 32
Modesty, 38-39
Moods, 17-18
Muscles, 6
Pee, 31, 55
Penis
    ejaculation, 31-32
    erections, 28-30
    size, 8
    touching, 25, 32, 42-44
Pimples, 11
Privacy in the bathroom, 39, 42
Private information, 9, 25, 29, 32, 33, 47-49
Private parts
    changes, 8
    pictures, 46
    touching, 24-25, 42-44

Puberty
  age that it begins, 4
  definition, 2
Pubic hair, 9
Public, 47
Rules
  public vs. private, 47-49
  safety, 38-44
  touching, 40-44
Safety rules, 38-44
Semen, 31-33, 55
Sexual feelings, 19-25, 56
Shaking hands, 44
Shaving, 10
Showering. **See** Hygiene
Skin care, 11
Smells, bad, 12-13
Sperm, 55
Sweethearts, 23-24
Testicles, 8, 25, 46
Touching rules, 40-44
Underarm hair, 9
Urinals, 39
Urine, 31, 55
Voice changes, 16
Washing. **See** Hygiene
Wet dreams, 33, 54
Zits, 11

About the Author

Terri Couwenhoven, M.S., is an AASECT certified sexuality educator who specializes in working with people who have intellectual disabilities, their families, and the professionals who support them.

She is the author of **The Girls' Guide to Growing Up: Choices & Changes in the Tween Years** and **Teaching Children with Down Syndrome about Their Bodies, Boundaries, and Sexuality: A Guide for Parents and Professionals,** as well as other publications. When she is not teaching, she is Clinic Coordinator for the Down Syndrome Clinic at Children's Hospital of Wisconsin.

Terri has two daughters; her oldest has Down syndrome.